Caroline P

C000000495

A CRYING SHAME

Vanguard Press

VANGUARD PAPERBACK

© Copyright 2021
Caroline Parkes

The right of Caroline Parkes to be identified as author of
this work has been asserted by her in accordance with the
Copyright, Designs and Patents Act 1988.

A CIP catalogue record for this title is
available from the British Library.

ISBN 978 1 78465 786 4

Vanguard Press is an imprint of
Pegasus Elliot MacKenzie Publishers Ltd.
www.pegasuspublishers.com

First Published in 2021

Vanguard Press
Sheraton House Castle Park
Cambridge England

Printed & Bound in Great Britain

Dedication

This book is dedicated to all those souls who were prepared to listen to my ideas and words from conception to completion. To them, I owe the greatest debt of gratitude.

Particular thanks go to my husband, Geoff Parkes, and my daughter, Georgina Ladd. Two people without whom I would be lost.

A WORD FROM THE AUTHOR

I was always a poet but, for a long time, no one told me that. I would write funny ditties on cards, for family and friends, but in my head I would construct rhymes around things that I cared about. Things that affected me. Sometimes those rhymes turned into quotes that I felt encompassed my thoughts.

But, I still didn't write poetry. Then, suddenly, two poems materialized on paper. *The Beggar's Parade* and *Those Fields*. And I found that I enjoyed writing them. They were not awe inspiring, none of my poetry is, but they had a pattern to them that worked for me and they said, in poetic form, what I couldn't easily express in conversation.

Years passed with two poems under my belt. A few more joined them, now and again, but then in 2017 I decided to join an open mic poetry group hosted by Shobana Patel, who founded The Soulful Group. I read some of my poems and suddenly, a passion for writing poetry consumed me.

At that first group meeting I was encouraged to be creative by Shobana. I was also fortunate enough to meet Fazana Kahtri, a woman who has become a good friend and who gave me the belief in myself to keep writing. Fazana introduced me to the poetry of

Mary Oliver and encouraged me to read her poem, *The Journey*. Once I had read it, I knew why. That poem continues to inspire me.

Most of my poems, to date, have rhythm. I have made an attempt at free verse, a couple of examples of which you will find at the end of this book for your consideration, but it isn't really my medium.

I was disappointed to google 'rhyming poetry' and find that it has something of a 'second rate' place in current trends. One poet, who shall remain nameless, said that he believed emotions cannot be expressed through rhyme. I don't agree with that. Depending on the rhythm chosen I believe that every emotion, from happiness, to anger, to sadness, to boredom, can be expressed with precision using the power of rhyme. But rather than call it rhyme, I prefer to call it 'rhythm'.

I will leave you to decide for yourself whether or not I'm right about that. Bear in mind that sometimes, you will need to work out the 'rhythm' for yourselves. It is not always immediately apparent.

Poetry allows me to express my version of reality. But please remember that reality is always in the eye of the beholder. I am not intending, in any way, to influence the views of others.

One further thing. The pictorial short poems reflect

the inspiration for the poems that follow. I always begin with an idea and those ideas form the foundation of my poetry. Some of them are different to the poems that follow, some of them are very similar. All have given rise to my thoughts.

Caroline Parkes.

Contents

ACKNOWLEDGMENTS

I would like to acknowledge two people in particular who, together, are completely responsible for this book being created, Shobana Patel and Fazana Khatri. The first poem in this book was inspired by them.

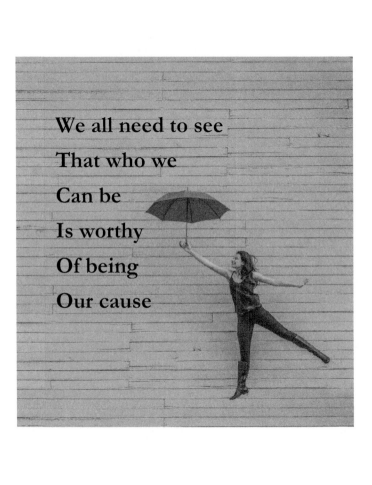

We all need to see
That who we
Can be
Is worthy
Of being
Our cause

Inspiration

Sometimes
There's something
Inside us
Something
That needs
A release
But sometimes
It's something
That never is
Found
So it's something
That never, is freed

But then there are times
To be fated
Times when a person
Appears
A person who gives
What we need
To receive
Then we see
What we need to
Believe

We don't need release
To be witnessed

We don't need
A round
Of applause
But we do need
To see
That who we
Can be
Is worthy of being
Our cause

Some just seek
Some notice
That they do
In fact
Exist
And are more
Than just
A faceless, nameless
'thing'
to be
Dismissed

The Beggar's Parade

The church stood unforgiving
As the congregation prayed
And the beggar came a calling
For the Armistice Parade

He was loud in condemnation
Cursing piety and sin
He disturbed the peace of plenty
That reigned glorious within

From the silence of Remembrance
Came the silent smell of waste
Came the silence of discomfort
Came the silence of distaste

Embarrassed to ignore him
Embarrassed to chastise
United in revulsion
The crowd withdrew their eyes

But one man in his wisdom
Saw no sinner in their midst
Just a poor man seeking notice
That he did, in fact, exist

He shouted from the pulpit
To the beggar in the aisle
'I see you, now be humble
Come rest your soul a while'

And with those words of wisdom
The beggar bowed his head
Nothing more he uttered
Nothing more he said

Until the final moments
When the veterans of the war
Passed his stagnant body
And paraded to the door

Then he rose in silence
Pinned the medals to his chest
And took his place beside them
A hero, like the rest

Children of the future
Need never feel the sun
For they live within
The darkness
Of the games
Just made
For one

Those Fields

I used to play upon those fields
Where now the planners play
Plotting their destruction
Whatever people say

Marking out the boundaries
For the buildings that will rise
Once the battle's over
And the final bluebell dies

A land of dreams and dragons
Bulldozed into dust
But planners call it progress
And progress says we must

We must destroy the grasslands
Where the children used to play
Clog the scene with concrete
And a cyber space café

For children of the future
Have no need for open space
Have no need to feel the freedom
Of the sun upon their face

There is safety in the buttons
Of the games that feed their minds
And the sword that slayed the dragon
Has been **fully,** redesigned

Sometimes, something beautiful
Will come into our lives
Then fade and gently pass away
Not destined to survive
For like the blossom of a rose
Whose beauty fades so fast
Sometimes, some things beautiful
Are never meant to last

Roots

The roots of old acquaintance
Lay buried in our past
Betwixt, between the daffodils
Down lanes that we have cast
Beside the running waters
In the rivers of our mind
Where friendship and forget-me-nots
Grow ever more entwined

Where memories are planted
That death cannot defeat
For death leaves no impression
Where the past and present meet
It's lost amongst the ripples
In the rivers of our mind
Where time is but a notion
That our hearts can leave behind

And I will find you there my friend
Laughing in the breeze
Speaking to me softly
In the rustling of the trees
Waiting by the waters
In the rivers of my mind
To watch the wind together
As it makes the past unwind

And what you had to teach me
Can be heard in all I say
Making you a part of me
Until my dying day
You'll always live within me
In the rivers of my mind
Until the currents carry me
To where our souls entwine

Babies are angels
Minus the wings
They're marvellous, magical
Miracle things
Blessed is the home
That captures their heart
For that's where the loveliest
Lovingness starts

The Dance

This poem is dedicated to my daughter, Georgina.

Once upon a time my love
Love danced a dance with me
And I believed, with all my heart
We'd dance eternally

But then the music changed my love
However hard I tried
I could no longer dance my love
And something fragile died

But you must never doubt my love
That dance you did not see
For though it could not last my love
That dance gave you, to me

And if I had my time again
I'd dance that dance once more
I'd let the music take my hand
And guide me to the floor

For as the music played my love
Your spirit came alive
Created something beautiful
That always will, survive

This painted smile
Is just a sham
That hides the truth
Of who I am

The Mask

I have a mask, I wear it well
So well that no one else can tell
What lies behind its bright façade
As I perform my sad charade
For all the world I must deceive
That no one ever, shall perceive
This painted smile is just a sham
That hides the truth, of who I am

I want to be the person
That life tells me
I can be
I want to be magnificent
I want to be
Set free

The Genie of the Bottle

The genie of the bottle
Has such confidence and flare
He is garrulous and vibrant
He is bold and debonair
Bewitching and beguiling
He promises the earth
If only I will sup with him
And revel in his mirth

His glass is never empty
For it's full of joie de vivre
And I want every drop of him
To be inside of me
I want to be the person
That he tells me I can be
I want to be magnificent
I want to be set free

He liberates my senses
With his captivating ways
And removes my inhibitions
With his subtle cabernets
Deliciously indulgent
Flirtatiously designed
He sets me on a journey
That will deconstruct my mind

Dismantle my defences
Leave me soulless and exposed
Dancing to a piper's tune
That someone else composed
With confidence abandoned
The prison walls descend
I've reached my destination
This is where my journey ends

Too late the veil is lifted
From my melancholy eyes
And I see the smoke and mirrors
The illusions and the lies
But in that maze of mayhem
I've forgotten who I am
I'm lost within a mirage
In the playground of the damned

The genie of the bottle
Has long crumbled into dust
Shattered the foundations
Upon which I built my trust
With vice like grip he holds me
And suddenly I see
I'll never be magnificent
I'll never be set free

Never try
To tell me
That I live
The way
I choose
Not until
You've
Trodden
In my shame
Encrusted
Shoes

Addiction

I'm addicted
I'm an addict
Past the point of no return
There's nothing more to help me
Nothing more that I can learn
This craving
This compulsion
This all-consuming curse
Will hound me till I'm dying
From it's crazy, quenchless, thirst

I've had my stint in rehab
Had it time and time again
I start to think I'm winning
Till they let me out
And then
This evil thing inside my brain
This demon takes control
And cheats me of my choices
As its hunger takes its toll

You can tell me
I'm a waster
That my habit is a crime
That I am just a parasite
Not worthy of your time
But never try to tell me
That I live the way I choose
Not until you've trodden
In my shame encrusted shoes

For those who live
With choices
Will never comprehend
That I have no ability
No faculty to mend
Something in me's broken
It's a part I can't replace
My next fix could be fatal
It's a fate I have to face

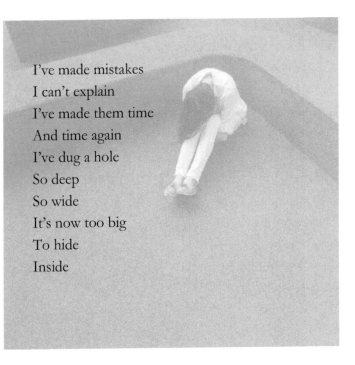

I've made mistakes
I can't explain
I've made them time
And time again
I've dug a hole
So deep
So wide
It's now too big
To hide
Inside

The System

You sell your love
For money
And a bag
Of crack cocaine
In a worthless
Vicious cycle
Where your dreams hold
No domain
Your mind is
Beyond caring
Your body's lost
Its will
You were born
Into a system
That demands
You pay the bill
You have to fill
Its coffers
If you want to
Learn to fly
But if your purse
Is empty
It will stand and
Watch you die

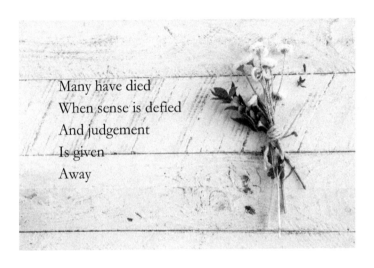

Many have died
When sense is defied
And judgement
Is given
Away

The Gambler

This poem is dedicated to the memory of Alastair Henry McLaren Munt, a good friend, who died at the hands of a drunk driver on the 16th December 2014. A man greatly missed.

I guess that we all
Have a weapon of choice
But you made the choice
To unlock it
When you stood at the bar
With your gin and a jar
And the key to your car
In your pocket

How did it feel
As you sat at the wheel
Did you think of the risk
Did you mock it?
Or did the power in your palm
To generate harm
Fight the wit in your wisdom
To stop it

As you drove out of town
Did your eyes let you down
Did your thoughts start
To wander away
Did your consciousness glide
Did your foot, slip and slide
Did your mind, just refuse, to obey?

Could it not comprehend
As you took that last bend
Where the flowers of remembrance lay
That many have died
When sense is defied
And judgment
Is given away

You ran out of luck
With the gamble you took
You played Russian roulette
And you lost
The dice didn't fall
To the sound of your call
And the end of my friend
Was the cost

But can I just ask
As I take you to task
Before I move on with my day
Did you get the notion
As wheels were in motion
That soon
You'd be called on
To pay

Called on to pay
Till your bones all decay
Long after your time
Has been spent
For whilst prison may punish
The guilt that will flourish
Will cover your soul
With his scent

They sell liberty
And freedom
At a price
I cannot pay
So they throw me
On the scrap heap
And they take them
Both away

In a World Where

I'm penniless and homeless
In a world where money rules
And the holders of the purse strings
Are all vagabonds and fools
They sell liberty and freedom
At a price I cannot pay
So they throw me on a scrap heap
And they take them both away

They leave me in the gutter
In a world that still believes
The homeless of our cities
Are all trespassers and thieves
Masters of deception
Directors of disguise
Out to fleece the future
With their falsehoods and their lies

How am I to answer
In a world that doesn't care
My plight is not their worry
My despair not their affair
In seeking absolution
They may offer me their pound
But it doesn't prick their conscience
That my body's on the ground

A hand out from a food bank
In a world that's grown obese
Won't alter my existence
Or cause suffering to cease
If you want to help me
Don't offer me a meal
Ask me how I'm struggling
Ask me how I feel

Don't judge me by my cover
In a world where beauty wins
But look beyond my vices
My addictions and my sins
See me as a person
Deserved of a choice
Give me back my dignity
Give me back my voice

I'm pleading with you
Begging
Just give me one
Last chance
Just give me
One more
Moment
To touch this world
And dance
I know my time
Is over
I know I have
To go
But one more
Precious moment
Could define me
As I go

The Gift of Goodbye

This poem is inspired by the story of Diane Pretty and all those who follow in her footsteps.

What judge has got
The right to rule
Whilst cloistered in
Some cold cocoon
On what should be
My final gift
To those who cherished
How I lived

To those who stood
And held my hand
Throughout each painful,
Anguished stand
And watched through
Hopeless, helpless eyes
As everything I am
Just died

It wasn't what
I saw for me
When I still had
My dignity
I fought for fate
To let me live
But fate has no more
Left to give

My body has
Just ceased to be
Its every moment
Tortures me
I want to be
Allowed to die
To orchestrate
My last goodbye

For that is all
I have to give
To those who cherished
How I lived
The gift of having
My embrace
As I drift to
Another place

It's not for me
I want the chance
To orchestrate
That final dance
But for the loves
I leave behind
That they should have
Some peace of mind

That they should know
I left the show
In peace as I
Had wished to go
And that when they
Remember me
They do it
With serenity

But sadly that
Can never be
That gift has been
Denied to me
The judges have
Removed my choice
Removed my will
Removed my voice

And oh I feel
Such abject rage
That I am forced
To be encaged
Inside this bloody
Useless shell
My living tomb
My living hell

Such rage that those
I love so much
Will be denied
My final touch
And in its stead
Will have to see
How brutal death
Can truly be

I ask again
Who has the right
To take from me
My last goodnight
To take away
The only worth
I have to give
To this fair earth

Maybe, we're all
An enigma
A mystery
No one
Can solve

But only with
Insight and wisdom
Will tolerance
Start to evolve

Enigma

This poem is inspired by the life of Alan Turing, who, on being convicted of indecency in 1952, was forced to undergo chemical castration. His offence was being in a loving relationship with another man, Arnold Murray. At the time, Turing is quoted as saying: 'No doubt I shall emerge from it all a different man, but quite who I am I have not found out.' He died from a suspected suicide in 1954.

They came for him
After he'd given
His heart
And his soul
To the war
An enigma
They just
Couldn't fathom
With secrets
They wouldn't
Ignore

His mind was the thing
That they'd wanted
And they'd taken
What that had
To give
So when it
Had served all
Its purpose
They severed
Its reason
To live

His sin was believing
In freedom
An absolute
Freedom
To live
With integrity
Born of a
Nature
And all that
A nature
Can give

But naivety led
To his downfall
Small minds
Couldn't duplicate
His
So they did
What they could
To conform him
To their own
Understanding
Of bliss

And as he looked
Into the future
He knew that he'd never
Be whole
He knew that
He'd always be
Different
In ways that
No life could
Console

And so, as we know
He chose dying
As better
Than living
The lies
As better than
Living
In pieces
Partitioned
behind some
Disguise

Too late we have sought
To forgive him
We pardon him
Now that he's dead
But the truth is
We all should
Have listened
To all that
Was done
And not said

Listened and known
We were erring
Listened
And sought
To be fair
For laws made
When life has departed
Are worthless
To those
Who aren't
There

His enigma now serves
To remind us
That all of us
Need to be
Heard
And all of us
Need to be
Free to be
True
And free to be free
As a bird

Turn to face the future
For it's those who
Stand and fight
That change the
World's perception
Of what's wrong
And what is right

Different

I can only wonder
What the world would be to me
If I had been the person
That life set me up to be
If I hadn't had to challenge
What so many would agree
Is how I would be better
If I'd sought conformity

If life had just acknowledged
In a way I understood
That I am just a person
Who is humble, kind and good
Then I'd be so different
I would now be living free
Instead of being imprisoned
In some crass hypocrisy

Where people offer platitudes
Declare an open mind
Then leave behind an attitude
That's cruel and unkind
All I ask, is see me
For the person that I am
Don't force me to exist within
Some soulless, empty, sham

I'm proud of what God made me
I'm how I'm meant to be
I cannot hide the simple truth
That I'm made differently
The freedom that I wanted
Seems too much for some to give
And so I have to contemplate
Just how I want to live

To live amongst the shadows
To be soulless and unknown
Or stand and face the future
Claim tomorrow as my own
I think I'll face the future
For it's those who choose to fight
That change the world's perception
Of what's wrong, and what is right

We don't know how
To manage
We don't know
What to do
We don't know how
To start to live
Without
The power
Of two

Soul Mates

We were partners
On a journey
Shared a thirst
For being alive
Had a hope
We'd go together
On that final
Fairground
Ride

But fate determined
Differently
And now I'm half
Of two
Left to muddle
Aimlessly
Without
The power
Of you

Our house once full
Of laughter
Has a melancholy
Air
It seems to be
In mourning
For the two
Who used
To share

Its silence has
The sadness
Of an empty
Broken shell
That's left with
Nothing more to give
And nothing more
To tell

There used to be
A Lover here
A Parent and
A Friend
A Companion
And a Colleague
An Accomplice
A Godsend

A Partner
And a Playmate
A Comrade
And a Chum
A secret sharing
Loving, caring
Undemanding
One

But all those roles
Once taken
Now stand vacant
And untouched
A lifetime of
Togetherness
Consigned
Unto the dust

It's not a state
Of being
That anyone
Would choose
And no one could
Or ever would
Begin to fill
Your shoes

Your shoes
That now stand empty
Bereft of all
Their zest
Bereft of that
Magnificence
That once, made me,
My best

I don't know how to
Deal with it
I don't know what
To do
I don't know how
To start to live
Without the power
Of two

There's clothes
Without a wearer
That I know
Will have
To go
Seedlings that
You planted
That I doubt
Will ever
Grow

Little jobs
Unfinished
That only you
Can do
All left as if
You're back to us
Before the day
Is through

Time will heal
They tell me
And I trust that
To be true
One day I'll smile
And chuckle
At the memories
Of you

But now,
Just in this
Moment,
It's a struggle
To survive
Surrounded by
The trappings
Of an amputated
Life

They say that stones
May break our bones
But words can never hurt us
How wrong they are
For bones
Will heal
But wounds
From words
Subvert us

Bully You

Look at her
The ugly witch
The feral children
Cried
Who would want
To be her friend
She is a bitch
They lied

They lied because
They saw in her
What they could not
Profess
A beauty
That is rarely seen
And rarer still
Possessed

Jealousy
Was hidden
Behind a mask
Of hate
Behind a mask
Of anger
That no sense
Could infiltrate

Their only means
Of dealing
With a better
Brighter star
Was to take away
Its sparkle
Leave it wounded
Hurt and scarred

They made her life
A living hell
They hounded her
To death
They took away her will
To live
They took away
Her breath

So sad that now
No one will see
How beautiful
She was
How beautiful
She would have been
A gem
The world has lost

They say that stones
May break our bones
But words
Can never hurt us
How wrong they are
For bones can heal
But wounds from words
Subvert us

Some never trust
A love that's free
So cage it
For
Eternity

Plastic People

Part 1: The Deception

Plastic people
Often say
I'll never try
To change the way
You walk, or talk
Or smell, or dress
It's all a lie
To woo, impress

It lures you in
It lures you on
It makes you feel
That you're the one
The one that God
Has surely blessed
For you have found
The very best

But then the little
Comments start
The little digs
That rip apart
That fragile corner
Of your soul
That should be growing
Strong, and whole

You start to wonder
Who you are
To question how
You came this far
How could this man
So great, so good
Be wanting you
When no one could

You think he's right
To rant and rave
You should be better
Should behave
If only you
Could get this right
Could get the picture
See the light

Then all your dreams
Would be fulfilled
His trust in you
Would be rebuilt
He wouldn't have
To lose control
And break more pieces
Of your soul

Part 2: The Truth

When will you learn
My little one
That this is nothing
You have done
This is a coward
Through and through
Who has to be
In charge of you

For Plastic People
Never see
The beauty of
What love can be
They never trust
A love that's free
So cage it, for
Eternity

Oh vanity of vanities
To think your love was mine
When it was simply gifted
For a precious piece of time

The love you gave grows cold now
You turn your back to go
You take away a piece of me
That I will never know

Not for me

Do you want me
To be different
To be something that
I'm not
To just accept
I'm worthless
Without changing
What I've got
To just become
An image
Of the person that
I'd be
If you conjured up
Perfection
And implanted it
In me

I'll never be
Your puppet
I'll always have my
Flaws
But now I see
With certainty
I can't be shaped
By yours
It doesn't mean

Perfection
That you seek will
Never be
It simply means
You're not the one
I'm looking for
For me

Don't take me
To the slaughter
Just because
You can
This life to me
Is precious
And I like the girl
I am

A Million Dollars

I felt a million dollars
In my tiny little dress
With my skimpy little top
And my hair a tousled mess
Like a model from the paper
On a fun filled, fuel filled night
Looking to be dancing
Till the early morning light

I didn't dress to lure you
I wasn't yours to take
I was a mother, and a lover
Not a woman on the make
I was out to just enjoy myself
Have a good weekend
Have fun again, be young again
Laugh again with friends

But you decided what I was
Not knowing who I am
And you decided I was just
A sacrificial lamb
You took me to the slaughter
And you slayed the girl I was
And I will never find again
That girl that I have lost

I wish that I could tell the world
I made you come undone
I can't because you played your card
You played your card, and won
That tiny little dress I had ?
That skimpy little top ?
It seems they've made the world believe
I chose
Just what I got

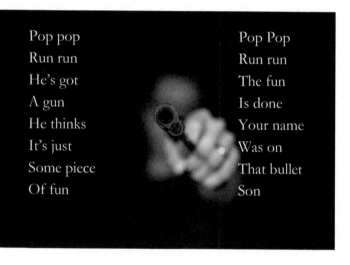

Pop pop
Run run
He's got
A gun
He thinks
It's just
Some piece
Of fun

Pop Pop
Run run
The fun
Is done
Your name
Was on
That bullet
Son

82

Adolescent Rage

A war is waging
In amongst
The tenements
And tower blocks
Where feral children
Roam in packs
And rule by fear
Their postcode patch

For gangsters of
This modern age
Are dressed in
Adolescent rage
A rage so raw
And unrefined
It's destined to
Destroy the mind

Destroy the mind
That learns from hoods
And videos
And Hollywood
That money talks
And money comes
From robberies
And stolen guns

And drugs of every
Type and kind
That stay the boredom
Of the mind
And take away
The cold remains
Of all ambition
From its veins

No future here
Is guaranteed
So no one pays
A moments heed
To what tomorrow
Has to give
It's just enough
To fight to live

For life is cheap
On ruthless streets
Where lawlessness
And anger meet
It only takes
One switchblade knife
To take another
Fledgling life

Another
Disenfranchised youth
Who dies before
He learns the truth
That life has so much
More to give
To those who find
The will to live

And we must not
Destroy that will
But must somehow
Some way, instil
A breath of life
Into those minds
Where still lies hope
To seek and find

For none so young
Should be ignored
Or left to rot
And be abhorred
Before we give it
Every shot
Throw everything
That we have got

To bring them back
From anarchy
Restore some sense
Of sanity
And give a purpose
To the lives
That we have
Rashly, bastardised

Glory seeks
To lure the brave
Before it dances
On their grave

I Can't Imagine

I can't imagine
Who believes
That war is not
A game of thieves
Where glory seeks
To lure the brave
Before it dances
On their grave

Where avaricious
Vultures fight
To claim a prize
Not theirs by right
Then hammer out
Their selfish deals
That keep alive
The Killing Fields

I can't imagine
Why it is
That we should just
Accept all this
Accept that lives
Are being lost
Without regard
To what it cost

Without regard
To girls and boys
Who only went
To play with toys
They didn't go
To 'Do or Die'
That was another
Soldier's cry

I can't imagine
Any more
There's any point
To any war
The time has come
To stand our ground
And ask to know
Who spends our pound

Ask why our taxes
Pay the bills
For wars that cannot
Cure our ills
For wars that no one
Wants to see
Except those skilled
In puppetry

I can't imagine
But I know
For video
Has stole the show
And shown us all
The darker side
Of how conceited
Leaders lied

There is no sin
In giving in
No slander to
Surrendering
Entrust the future
To the bold
Who seek to break
The devil's hold

Morality is neutral
It has no faith or creed
It comes from simple decency
That every human needs
Religion cannot change that
It cannot make it right
For anyone
To ever seek
To take another's
Life

No Place Here

What part
Of being human
Could you just not
Comprehend
That you chose
To shoot a stranger
Who had nothing
To defend

You have no place
In my world
You're an empty
Worthless shell
Destined to be buried
In some living
Lifeless
Hell

Childhood is
A dream denied
To tortured souls
Who try and hide
Behind the imagery
Of youth
That's seen too much
Of brutal truth

Tortured

When all the bombs
Began to fall
You saw the carnage
Saw it all
Saw generations
Lose their lives
Before your tortured
Tear filled eyes

There never was
A warning bell
As tortured towns
Were turned to hell
And mortars shelled
To barest bone
The only world
You'd ever known

You saw its pain
You heard its screams
You hear them still
They haunt your dreams
And if you should
Just close your eyes
You'll hear again
Its tortured cries

You'll see again
Each chilling scene
As homes were bombed
To smithereens
By men who never
Knew who died
Or loved the scapegoats
Trapped inside

Your tortured tears
All fell in vain
There was no sunshine
After rain
No future that
Could justify
Why just so many
Had to die

What innocence
Could ever last
With such a tortured
Butchered past
More likely that
It turns to hate
Another soul
To liquidate

Your childhood was
A dream denied
For tortured souls
Can never hide
Behind the imagery
Of youth
That's been exposed
To brutal truth

Home provides
That gifted chance
To grow our wings
And learn
To dance

Home

No child should ever
Feel alone
Within the boundaries
Of their home

For there should be
The loving arms
That shelter them
From hidden harms

And listen to
Their hopes and fears
Whilst wiping dry
Their childhood tears

The only demons
They should dread
Are those they conjure
In their head

Which loving winds
Will chase away
Like clouds
Upon a summer's day

For home should be
Their gifted chance
To grow their wings
And learn to dance

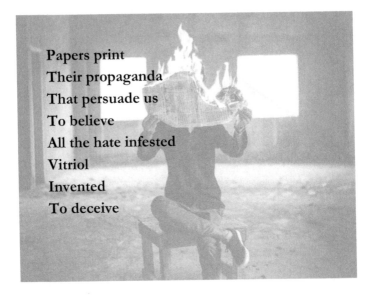

Papers print
Their propaganda
That persuade us
To believe
All the hate infested
Vitriol
Invented
To deceive

This Bride

This is only one possibility of reality, in a world full of alternatives.

This bride was never
Dressed in white
Or bathed in early
Morning light
Or walked with pride
Down flowered aisles
To loving smiles

She wasn't fated
Loved and blessed
Or gently wooed
And then caressed
For she was marked
A soldier's whore,
To feed the war

To serve the men
And be controlled
Become a chattel
Bought and sold
As breeding stock
To fill the ranks,
And all those tanks

And in her childish
Make-believe
She saw no motive
To deceive
But who in truth
Can really say,
She chose this way

For choice depends
On being free
To lift the veil
Of trickery
And make decisions
Based on facts,
Not Google's scraps

And when one stops
To contemplate
The cruel hand
Of twisted fate
Do we not also bear
Some blame,
Some twisted shame

For is this bride
Not yet being played
By writers who
Are being paid
To feed the politics
Of hate,
They infiltrate

Let's rise above
The bigotry
The venom
The hypocrisy
And seek to see
Just where she stands
When she is back,
On these fair lands

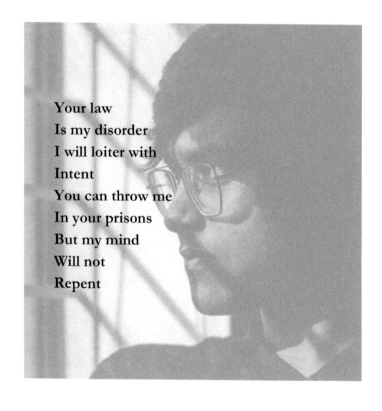

Your law
Is my disorder
I will loiter with
Intent
You can throw me
In your prisons
But my mind
Will not
Repent

Finding Heaven

This is a poem in memory of Oscar Martinez and his young daughter, Angie, who died attempting to cross the Rio Grande from Mexico to the US, and to all of the thousands of others who have died seeking sanctuary.

They died as the sun
Was fading
On a glorious
Afternoon
A father and daughter
Together
Chasing the eye of
The moon

Chasing the dreams
Of the tortured
Whilst living the life
Of the damned
Approaching the borders
Of heaven
By the side of
The Rio Grande

And there from the edge
They could see it
The start of
The yellow brick road
Paved with the promise
Of freedom
And the flowers that free men
Had sown

They saw in that moment
Their future
And they saw how their future
Could be
And they knew that this time
Was their moment
It was time to be
Finally free

And so they launched into
The water
Embarked on that last
Fatal ride
Risked all that they had
For a future
For a life on the sunnier
Side

But children in trouble
They struggle
This wasn't a pool
By the Med
It was torrents of turbulent
Water
Spiralling over their
Head

He did what he could to
Protect her
He wanted them both
To survive
But when she was lost
To the river
He chose then to die
By her side

And so they made heaven
Together
Arrived at the very
Same time
But couldn't it all
Have been different
If freedom was never
A crime

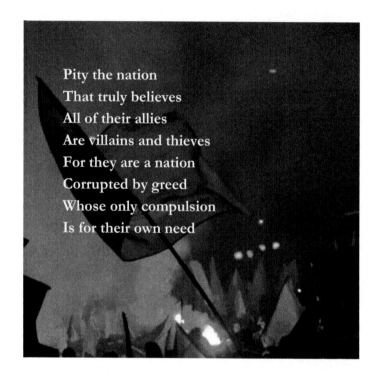

Pity the nation
That truly believes
All of their allies
Are villains and thieves
For they are a nation
Corrupted by greed
Whose only compulsion
Is for their own need

End of an Empire

There is no future for us now
The western world must take its bow
The final curtain call has come
There is no more that can be done
We had our chance
We tried and failed
All hope has gone
That ship has sailed
We gave it everything we had
But everything we had,
Turned bad

We're living now on borrowed time
Supremacy is in decline
And victims of our ardent greed
Are fighting back and planting seeds
Of hate that will
In time begin
To flourish
And become fulfilled
We gave it everything we had
But everything we had,
Turned bad

There's little left worth fighting for
Let's wave the flag, concede the war
Morality has gone off course
And lawlessness is now in force
It's what we pay
For losing sight
Of what is wrong
And what is right
We gave it everything we had
But everything we had,
Turned bad

Another order now will rise
An order that we'll all despise
We won't agree with what they do
Or how they dictate me, and you
We had our chance
We tried and failed
All hope has gone
That ship has sailed
We gave it everything we had
But everything we had,
Turned bad

We're nothing but a football
In some egocentric game
And those who we elected now
Should hang their heads
In shame

Passing the Baton

Our leaders have no judgment
And we've ceased to really care
A game show host excites us
So it's them we put up there
We give them what they want
From us
We vote for them
To be
A platform for the madness
That will crush both you and me

We watch them as they rise to fame
We follow them on tour
We raise the roof with battle cries
Our patronage secure
And if they break
A promise
Do we really give
A fig
When all we want's a ticket
To their hedonistic gig

For truth holds no temptation
It's devoid of any fun
False hope and wishful thinking
Is how the race is won
A moment of
Delusion
Is enough to keep us
Keen
And credentials hold no value
In a world that's crass, and mean

But when the party's over
And the revellers are gone
Together with the madness
That their greed has fed upon
What will we be
Faced with
What rubble
Will remain
Will there even be a future
For our children to regain

Or will we be discarded
Like the debris on the floor
Just the remnants of a circus
Not performing any more
A scattered chunk
Of wreckage
Left abandoned and
Forlorn
Searching for a life raft
In the centre of a storm

We need to clear our vision
Take the roses from our eyes
Shatter our illusions
And expose the fatal lies
For we have
Obligations
There's a baton in our
Hand
And future generations need
To know we made our stand

To know that in conclusion
We came to comprehend
The need to stand together
And endeavour to defend
A world that's being
Threatened
By a narcissistic
Gang
Who promise us Arcadia
Whilst letting justice hang

We need to rise together
Let our leaders understand
That bygone days are over
There's another 'coming' planned
Let's listen to each
Other
Let's take another
Tack
Let's joust with sense and reason
And let's take the future back

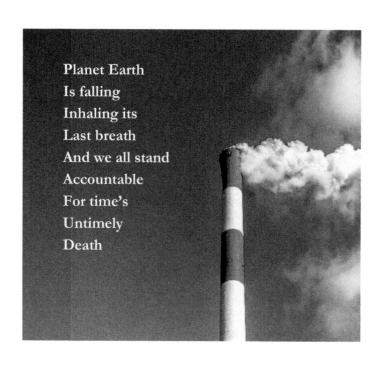

Planet Earth
Is falling
Inhaling its
Last breath
And we all stand
Accountable
For time's
Untimely
Death

The Dying Game

They're tearing down
The forests
For they want to use
The land
And the world stands by
Just watching
Too inert to raise
Its hand
Too self-centred
And unsighted
To be bothered
To complain
Too believing that
The future
Is a shoo-in
To remain

One morning
We'll discover
That the world has had
Enough
And we'll find the planet
Dying
Too polluted by
Our stuff
Then we'll don our

Dismal mantle
Wear our widows' weeds
Of shame
For all of us
Are players
In this, the dying
Game

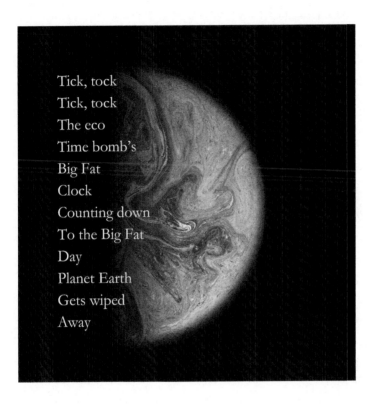

Tick, tock
Tick, tock
The eco
Time bomb's
Big Fat
Clock
Counting down
To the Big Fat
Day
Planet Earth
Gets wiped
Away

Plastic

We've so much
Bloody plastic
That we don't know
What to do
It throttles the
Environment
And sticks to sea
Like glue
It's persuasive
And pervasive
And it holds us
In its thrall
By our need to
manufacture
In the cheapest way
Of all

We're addicted to
Its presence
We love the things
It brings
In pretty glossy
Packages
With pretty glossy
Frills
We discard it

In a moment
Lob it straight in to
The bin
Or leave it
To be taken
By a cold, uncaring
Wind

Yet every piece
Discarded
Is the legacy
We leave
That someone
Somewhere
Someday
Will never quite
believe

Conclusion:

No one wakes up normal
We're all a tad insane
That's the beauty, and the magic
Of the now, outdated, brain

Funny Old World

It's a funny old world
We've arrived at
Where nothing is quite
As it seems
It's all a bit mad
Round the edges
And falling apart
At the seams
It looks like a world
I remember
But the word I remember
Was sane
And now it seems oddly
Peculiar
In a way that my brain
Can't explain

Is it me or has lunacy
Landed
Has absurdity taken
Control
Has a new definition of
Normal
Been embraced, taken root
And just grown
I used to believe that

The future
Is where our redemption
Would lie
For I never imagined
A future
Where our minds would be
Hung out
To dry

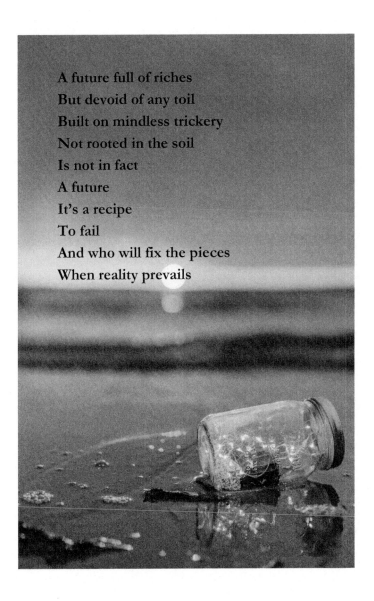

A future full of riches
But devoid of any toil
Built on mindless trickery
Not rooted in the soil
Is not in fact
A future
It's a recipe
To fail
And who will fix the pieces
When reality prevails

Instagram

You influence
The children
Who are coming up
Behind
You show them how
To desecrate
A bright and fertile
Mind
You make them want
To be you
You make them want
To live
In a world of
Puffed up pouting
That has nothing real
To give

What are you
Creating
What worth do you
provide
What will you look
Back upon
With real, deserved
Pride
A bundle of

Mementos
From an artificial
Past
That no one really
Cares about
And couldn't ever
Last

Or will your gift to
Children
Who you lure into your
Net
Be to make them all your
Puppets
Your adoring
Marionettes
Trick them into
Thinking
That they'll never have
To work
For life owes them
A living
And the grafters are
The jerks

When will we
Acknowledge
That this world of ours
Was built
On the backs of
Humble workers
On their failures and
Their guilt
On the madness
And the sadness
Of the men who
Without fuss
Made the world we take
For granted
Then bequeathed it all
To us

I'll take my chance
With happenstance
Kick off my shoes
And join the dance

I Don't Believe

This poem does not in any way reject spirituality.

I don't believe in angels
And I don't believe in God
For I believe religion
Was created as a rod
A rod to beat the people
Who can undermine the will
Of those who crave
To dominate
With all
Devouring
Skill

To cauterize the masses
Stop them spreading their disease
Of liberty and freedom
That would clamour for release
In poverty and slavery
With charters of despair
Your God restrains
As good as chains
And keeps them
Praying
There

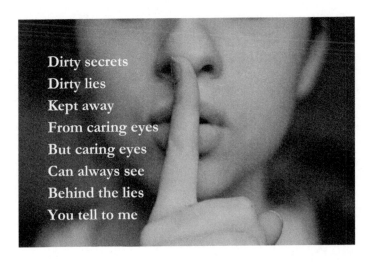

Dirty secrets
Dirty lies
Kept away
From caring eyes
But caring eyes
Can always see
Behind the lies
You tell to me

The following two poems reflect how abuse is sometimes not how you expect it to be. Whilst it must be terrible to be the victim of abuse, it must also be terrible to be accused of abuse that you have not, actually, committed.

999

I was nine
When daddy came
And burrowed down
Inside my bed
He burrowed down
So very deep
That now he's burrowed
In my head

He said it was
A kind of love
That only daddy's
Understood
And I his little
Fledgling bird
Believed his every
Single word

How could such
Tenderness be wrong
Such gentleness
Just not belong
To caring hands
That I could hold
Depend upon,
Till I grew old

So I believed that
Fragile touch
That I had come to trust
So much
Was something
Beautiful and pure
And I was captured
In its lure

But age with time
Begins to see
What wickedness
Was done to me
What innocence
Was ripped apart
Then left in shreds
Within my heart

In shreds that now
Will never heal
With scars that only
Just conceal
The open wounds
That still remain
Ingrained within
My fragile brain

Name and Shame

You named me
And you shamed me
And you took my life
Away
The moment that
You printed
What that liar
Had to say

It was just
An allegation
That the future would
Find false
But the future had
No part to play
When I became
A nonce

I know you had
A job to do
A paper to be
Sold
But did you give
A thought to what
Perhaps, you could
Withhold?

I hadn't been
Convicted
I wasn't a
Bad man
But words became
Imprinted
Made it look
As if
I am

Made it look
As if I did it
As if all her words
Were true
As if I were
A paedophile
Just wicked
Through and through

You told them
Where to find me
You gave them
My address
You threw me
To a throng of wolves
And gave me
No redress

How can that
Be justice?
How can that
Be fair?
And how do I
Begin to feel
That I'll be safe
'Out there'?

People make
Assumptions
They read
And they decide
That I'm worthy
Of attention
Of being loathed
And vilified

They feel that they're
Entitled
To treat me
With contempt
And even worse
To threaten me
With things
I can't
Prevent

And all the
Information
For the hatred that
They hold
Came from your
Creation
From the version
That you
Sold

I guess you know
It's over?
I was innocent
You see
I simply
Hadn't done it
It was all some
Fantasy

But still
I serve a sentence
A sentence with
No end
For some will always
Still believe
I'm destined
To offend

Forever
Is never
An option
Gifted to
Any of
Us

Dementia

Death came
But oh so slowly
Creeping through
Your brain
Taking you
In fragments
Till just a void
Remained

A void once filled
With loveliness
And every sort
Of care
And I so want
That person back
That's with me
But not there

Where the Hell

Where the hell
Are we going
Does it matter
We're running
Late?
Is something
So really important
It's something
That just
Cannot wait

Let's face it
If we died
Tomorrow
The world would
Continue
To turn
And that is the truth
We must nurture
A truth that
We all need
To learn

We all need
To learn
That living
Is never a gift
To be rushed
For forever is never
An option
Gifted to
Any of us

So take time
To smell
The flowers
Meander
The meadows
Of life
And if we don't
Make it
Tomorrow
Be assured that
The world
Will survive

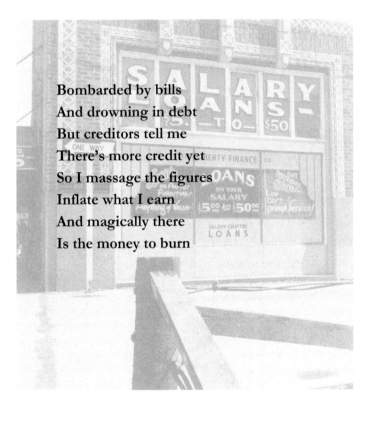

Bombarded by bills
And drowning in debt
But creditors tell me
There's more credit yet
So I massage the figures
Inflate what I earn
And magically there
Is the money to burn

Debt

Your life's on the brink
And you're drowning in debt
And yet all you can think of
Is what you can get
If you trade in the car
And you take out a loan
And you buy a new contract
To get a new phone

The rent's in arrears
And the bar bill is due
You paid your best friend
With a blank I.O.U.
Your card's at its max
You're in red at the bank
There's nothing to eat
And no gas in the tank

The post lays unopened
You bury your head
The bleep of the mobile
Is something to dread
Tomorrow you'll sit
And develop a plan
A method of paying
The best that you can

But tomorrow brings bills
That you find you'd forgot
And they'll never be paid
From a cold, empty pot
So you fill in a form
For another reprieve
And more of the plastic
That acts to deceive

That gives you a breather
And lets you pretend
That soon all this madness
Will come to an end
That some magical,
Marvellous, miracle cure
Will solve all your troubles
And make you secure

That never will happen
You're out of your depth
You'll never escape
From a spiral of debt
It will cover you, smother you
Leave you bereft
Believing that nothing
Worth living, is left

Just open your eyes
And lift up your head
Wherever there's life
Hope is never quite dead
Open the letters
Pick up the calls
It's silence that gives us
Those bricks in the walls

An Attempt at Free Verse

For your consideration.

Message from a Mistress

From where I stand
I gaze towards the lighthouse
And I see your wife
Standing with dignity
Impassive and immovable
Guiding you towards
Safe harbour

And far below
I see myself
The jagged rocks
Upon whose pinnacle
You gouge your very soul
Which then like flotsam
Floats adrift
And useless

Heed her warning
Come no closer
For I shall wreck you
And whilst I will survive
I know within my heart
That you
Would not

The Wedding Song

We will share time
Till death defeats us
But we will also
Give time,
And give space
For true love
Needs time,
And space,
To breathe

We will share
The end of the day,
But not always the day
We will have the last dance,
But not every dance

We will stand,
Side by side together,
But not so close together
That if one stumbles
The other falls
For the other
Must be free
To catch the pieces

We will live,
Together, for ever,
In the knowledge
That our lives
Are better,
For having the other,
With us

Printed in Great Britain
by Amazon

10932461R00088